ABSOLUTE BEGINN

Classical
Guitar

WISE PUBLICATIONS

London/New York/Paris/Sydney/
Copenhagen/Berlin/Tokyo/Madrid

Exclusive Distributors:
Music Sales Limited
14/15 Berners Street,
London W1T 3LJ, England.

Music Sales Corporation
257 Park Avenue South
New York
NY10010, USA.

Music Sales Pty Limited
20 Resolution Drive,
Caringbah, NSW 2229,
Australia.

Order No. AM972598
ISBN: 0-7119-9180-4
This book © Copyright 2003 by Wise Publications

Written and arranged by Gerald Goodwin
Music Processed by Simon Troup
Edited by Sorcha Armstrong
Book design by Chloë Alexander
Cover and text photographs by George Taylor
Featured guitar made by Christopher Dean
Model: Helen Sanderson

CD recorded and mastered by Jonas Persson

Printed in the United Kingdom

Your Guarantee of Quality:
As publishers, we strive to produce every book to the highest
commercial standards. This book has been carefully designed to
minimise awkward page turns and to make playing from it a real
pleasure. Particular care has been given to specifying acid-free,
neutral-sized paper made from pulps which have not been
elemental chlorine bleached. This pulp is from farmed sustainable
forests and was produced with special regard for the environment.
Throughout, the printing and binding have been planned to
ensure a sturdy, attractive publication which should give years of
enjoyment. If your copy fails to meet our high standards, please
inform us and we will gladly replace it.

Got any comments?
e-mail **absolutebeginners@musicsales.co.uk**

www.musicsales.com

Contents

Introduction

Welcome to *Absolute Beginners Classical Guitar*! Whether you already play guitar, or have never picked it up before, this book will show you everything you need to know to begin playing in the classical guitar style. Here you will find out how to tune up, read music and tablature, and start playing some well-known tunes on the guitar.

Using a progressive approach, you will quickly become familiar with:

• Written music and musical terms
• The **p i m a** fingerstyle system
• Apoyando and tyrando technique
• Reading and understanding tablature
• Playing simple chords and melodies

Although this book has been designed primarily for classical guitar you can also use it with an electric or acoustic guitar. However if you really want to play pop or rock music, I would suggest you also buy a copy of *Absolute Beginners Guitar*.

On the CD are professionally-recorded demonstrations of all the music and exercises in the book, plus a backing track for you to play along with as you learn.

Practise regularly and often. Twenty minutes every day is far better than two hours at the weekend with nothing in between. Not only are you training your brain to understand how to play the guitar and read music, you are also teaching your muscles to memorise certain repeated actions.

Let's get started!

This picture shows a typical classical guitar.

The classical guitar differs from a standard steel string acoustic in two important ways:

• Wider Neck
The neck is made wider to allow solo tunes to be played clearly with harmonies.

• Nylon Strings
The strings are made of nylon rather than steel to help project a warm deep sound.

History

The classical guitar has been around for over 150 years. In that time masters such as Barrios, Segovia and more recently John Williams (below), have all helped to establish it as a highly expressive instrument, easily capable of holding an audience spellbound with its range of harmonic possibilities.

headstock

tuning pegs

nut

frets

fingerboard

neck

strings

rosette

soundhole

body

saddle

bridge

Know your guitar

The headstock has six tuning pegs, three each side.

The tuning pegs are also known as machine heads, and consist of a metal capstan and a cog to tension the string.

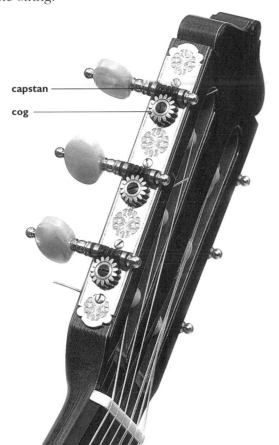

The soundhole on a classical guitar is usually more ornate than on an acoustic, with a 'rosette' around it.

Some have mother of pearl inlays or carving, but most have a pattern of some sort.

The fretboard has metal fret wires at intervals across it, and strings running along it.

The strings are kept in place by the nut as they leave the headstock.

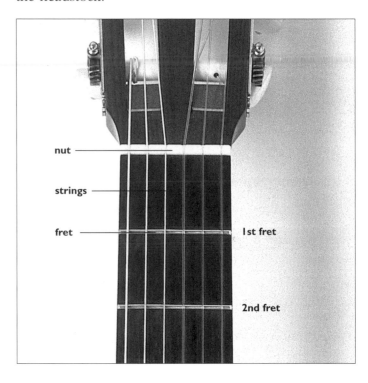

Follow these simple guidelines to make sure that you always feel comfortable while playing, and that you use the correct position.

• Your arms should never take the weight of the guitar – make sure it is resting comfortably on your legs.

• Don't let the neck point down towards the ground – the optimum angle should be about 45° (see photo).

• Make sure you don't tilt the guitar towards you to see the strings – rather, you should lean over it.

• Your chair and footstool should be adjusted so that you are comfortable sitting on the chair with your footstool raising your foot off the ground.

• The guitar should be tucked in between your legs.

Here is a photo of correct posture – using the footstool to raise the left foot, with the guitar tucked in between the legs.

Bend over the guitar to see the strings, rather than turn it towards you.

The footstool is the only other essential piece of equipment (apart from your guitar!) so make sure it's at the right height for you to feel comfortable.

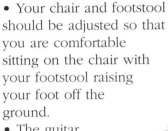

Right hand position

Here's a step-by-step illustration of the correct playing position for your right hand.

If you're left-handed follow these instructions for your left hand.

1 Rest your forearm lightly on the guitar.

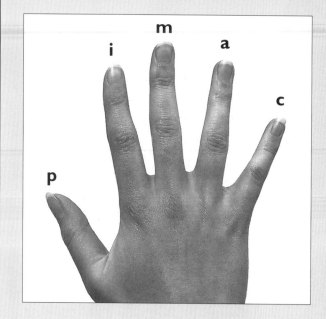

Why "pima"?

The 'pima' system derives from the spanish and has become standard throughout the classical world.

p stands for 'pulgar' – the thumb

i stands for 'indice' – the index

m stands for 'medio' – the middle

a stands for 'anular' – the ring finger

and **c** stands for 'cuatro' – the little finger, or fourth finger.

2 Arch your wrist so your fingers are approximately at 60 degrees to the back of your hand, then relax them so they become slightly curved.

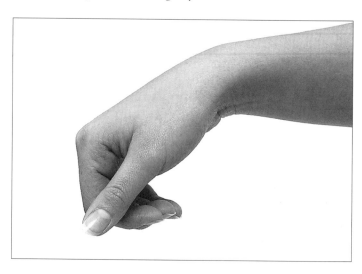

3 Place your thumb (**p**) on the 6th string. It will play the 6th, 5th and 4th strings.

4 Place your index finger (**i**) on the 3rd string, your middle finger (**m**) on the 2nd string, and your ring finger (**a**) on the 1st string, keeping your fingers curved. Your little finger is not always used so does not rest on any string.

Here's how to start using your left hand to fret individual notes.

Keep the hand and wrist relaxed and keep the thumb roughly vertical behind the neck, and roughly between the first and second fingers.

Don't let your wrist drop, like this:

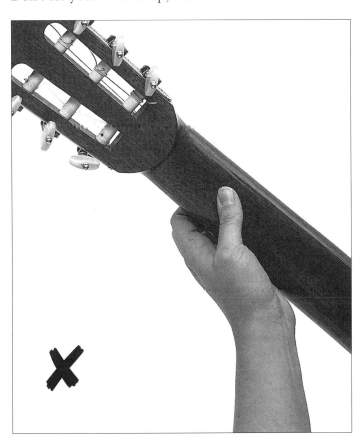

Use the one-finger-per-fret rule and place your fingers down on the guitar fretboard in between the metal fret wires.

Each finger has a different number, corresponding to numbers in guitar tablature. You will learn more about guitar tablature later, but for now, remember that on your left hand, your thumb is not used, your first finger = 1, and so on.

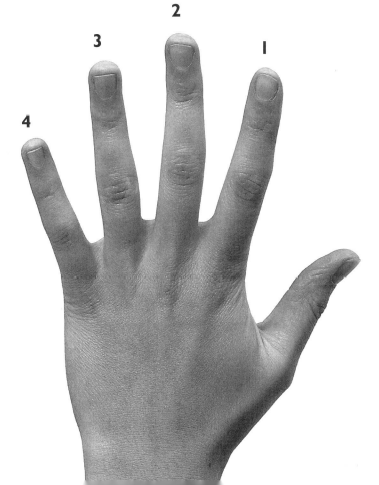

Tuning

Before you can start playing (and before each practice session) you should tune your guitar properly. There are plenty of ways to do this, so you should choose the one you find the easiest.

1 Use our CD
On **Track 1** of the CD with this book we've supplied tuning notes for each string, starting with the low E string and going upwards. Listen to the note produced, and try and match it to the note on the CD. Turn the tuning peg to loosen the string if you think it's too high, and tighten the string if you think it's too low.

2 Use an electronic tuner
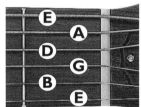
These are reasonably inexpensive and can be purchased from any music shop. Plug your guitar into it, pluck the string you want to tune, and check the dial – it should line up in the middle.
Other tuners may have a digital display, but generally, they will all tell you when it's in tune.

3 Tune to a keyboard
If you have a piano or keyboard, or if you're playing in a group, you should tune up to that, as it has a fixed pitch.

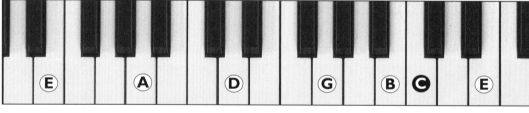

6th to 5th string	5th to 4th string	4th to 3rd string	3rd to 2nd string	2nd to 1st string
E A D G B E	E A D G B E	E A D G B E	E A D G B E	E A D G B E

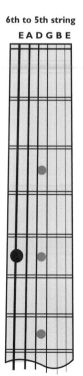  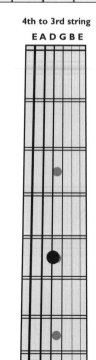 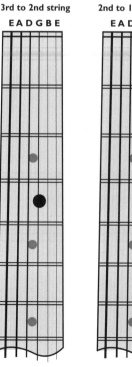

4 Tune the guitar to itself (relative tuning)
Most guitarists use this method – it's the most straightforward and reliable, if you're playing by yourself. However, you have to assume that the E string is in tune (unless you can tune it to something), so it may not be the most accurate way.

Play the note at the fifth fret on the E string – it should sound the same as the open A string. Continue in the same way for the other strings.

In order to play well it is important to develop good right hand finger co-ordination. Here's your first exercise. Support the neck of the guitar with your left hand, even though you won't be fretting any notes.

Your thumb should pluck the bottom E, A and D strings

Your fingers should pluck the G, B and top E strings

Rest your right hand fingers on the strings in the positions you've just learnt, slightly curled. Now try plucking the strings in order, using the method of plucking from the finger joint and not from the hand.

Your thumb (**p**) should pluck the bottom E string (the thickest string), the A string and the D string. Your index finger (**i**) should then pluck the G string (the third string), your middle finger (**m**) should pluck the B string (the second string) and your ring finger (**a**) should pluck the top E string. The correct position for each finger is shown on the left.

Repeat this exercise as many times as you like until you feel comfortable with the movement. It is very important to move the fingers from the knuckle joint and not by moving the whole hand. Keep the hand steady above the strings, in a slightly curled position.

Here is the exercise you've just played, written down using tablature. You will learn how to read this later in the book.

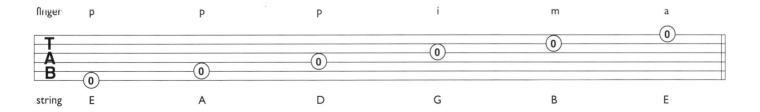

Tirando and apoyando

The two styles of playing that you need to become familiar with are called tirando and apoyando – translated as 'free stroke' and 'rest stroke'. These styles are used by both the thumb and fingers.

The free stroke (tirando)

This is generally used for accompaniment, chord playing and arpeggios (broken chords). Put simply, you pluck the string and let it ring out, probably in the way you have been doing up to now. Technically, you use all of the joints in your finger and thumb, to make a 'claw', which you use to pluck the string.

Here, the first finger presses on the third string…

▲ **Preparation**

…and plucks. Notice how the string is left to ring out.

✳ Active joint

▲ **Completion**

The rest stroke (apoyando)

The rest stroke is used mainly for melodies and emphasising single notes. Instead of letting the note ring out after plucking the string, you stop it slightly by pressing the finger down onto the next string. With the rest stroke, use only the knuckle joint to move the finger (see photo).

Here, the thumb presses on the sixth string…

▲ **Preparation**

…and immediately after plucking it, comes to rest on the fifth string.

✳ Active joint

▲ **Completion**

Here's your first exercise to get you used to reading and playing from tablature, and to give your right hand a little workout! It's very simple – there's one exercise for each string on the guitar.

Start with the top (thinnest) string, and pluck the open string four times. Then, press down behind the first fret with the first finger of your left hand,

and pluck the same string again. The note should sound higher than before. Continue up to the third fret. For the right hand, alternate plucking the string using the first and second fingers (**i** and **m**), using a steady rhythm.

The numbers underneath the tab are there for counting – it's not as complicated as it looks.

Top E String

0	0	0	0	1	1	1	1	2	2	2	2	3	3	3	3
i	m	i	m	i	m	i	m	i	m	i	m	i	m	i	m
1	2	3	4	1	2	3	4	1	2	3	4	1	2	3	4

B String

0	0	0	0	1	1	1	1	2	2	2	2	3	3	3	3
i	m	i	m	i	m	i	m	i	m	i	m	i	m	i	m
1	2	3	4	1	2	3	4	1	2	3	4	1	2	3	4

G String

0	0	0	0	1	1	1	1	2	2	2	2	3	3	3	3
i	m	i	m	i	m	i	m	i	m	i	m	i	m	i	m
1	2	3	4	1	2	3	4	1	2	3	4	1	2	3	4

D String

0	0	0	0	1	1	1	1	2	2	2	2	3	3	3	3
i	m	i	m	i	m	i	m	i	m	i	m	i	m	i	m
1	2	3	4	1	2	3	4	1	2	3	4	1	2	3	4

A String

0	0	0	0	1	1	1	1	2	2	2	2	3	3	3	3
i	m	i	m	i	m	i	m	i	m	i	m	i	m	i	m
1	2	3	4	1	2	3	4	1	2	3	4	1	2	3	4

E String

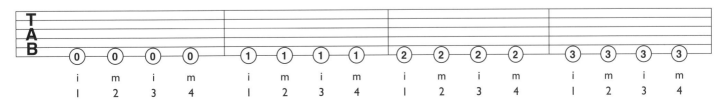

0	0	0	0	1	1	1	1	2	2	2	2	3	3	3	3
i	m	i	m	i	m	i	m	i	m	i	m	i	m	i	m
1	2	3	4	1	2	3	4	1	2	3	4	1	2	3	4

Reading music made easy

Shown on these two pages are the basic outlines of reading and understanding written music. You will learn more as we go along, but for now you will need to familiarise yourself with the concepts of pitch and rhythm, in order to read the music on the following pages.

The Stave

The music we play is written on five equally spaced lines called a stave or staff. It has five horizontal lines and looks like this:

Staves are divided into bars (or measures) by the use of a vertical line called a bar. Each bar has a fixed number of beats in it. A beat is the natural tapping rhythm of a song. Most songs have four beats in each bar, and we can tap our feet or count along with these songs.

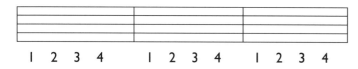

Occasionally, there are three beats in each bar, and we count like this:

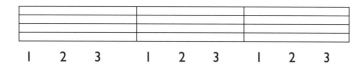

Time Signatures

At the beginning of every piece of music there are two numbers, written one above the other. This is called a time signature. The top number tells us how many beats are in a bar. The lower number tells us the value of these beats as expressed in the musical notation (this will be explained shortly).

The two most common time signatures in popular music are these:

4/4 is often shown as C, or Common Time.

Once given, the time signature is not repeated, unless the beat changes within a song. This happens only rarely in popular music.

Clefs

The other symbol we find at the beginning of each stave is called the treble clef. This fixes the pitch of the notes on the stave. The line that passes through the centre of the spiral, second up from the bottom, fixes the note G. The letter names for the lines and spaces are shown here:

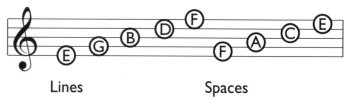

Lines   Spaces

Repeat signs

In music there are various standard markings which can be used to abbreviate the layout.
When we come to this sign:

it tells us to go back to where this sign appears:

(or sometimes when this does not appear, we return to the beginning) and repeat the section.

Note values

Now we come to notes and their time values. The notes tell the player exactly what to play, how to play it, and when to play it.

Semibreve (or whole note):

Minim (or half note):

Crotchet (or quarter note):

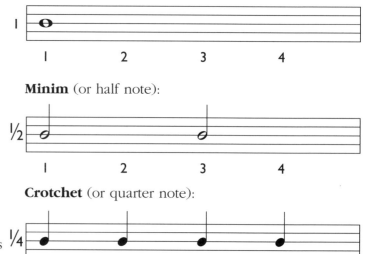

Quaver (or eighth note):

Semi-quaver (or sixteenth note):

The notes in each diagram above all add up to 4 beats, the beat being 1 crotchet. Quavers and semi-quavers are joined together with 'beams' to make the music tidier.

So in a piece of music in 4/4 time we count 4 beats to the bar, each beat being 1 crotchet:

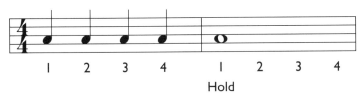

A bar in 2/4 time will contain 2 crotchet beats per bar:

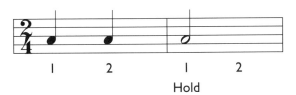

The same principle applies to 3/4 time:

Dotted notes
Above, we see a minim with a dot after it. The dot increases the time value of any note after which it is placed by half its original duration.

So, a dotted minim: 2 beats + 1 beat = 3 beats. A dotted crotchet: $1 + \frac{1}{2} = 1\frac{1}{2}$ beats.

Counting
Many guitar accompaniments consist of playing 8 quavers to each bar of 4/4 time. We still count 4 crotchets but to maintain an easy rhythm we count 1 + 2 + 3 + 4 +, each syllable being one quaver:

We can break this counting down further, so with semi-quaver rhythms the count would be: 1e+a 2e+a 3e+a 4e+a, each syllable being one semi-quaver:

Sometimes we see dotted quavers and semiquavers joined together. Again we count four, but the rhythm does not flow smoothly as with 8 quavers to the bar, and we count like this:

Rests
Just as notes tell us when to play, we have rests which tell us when not to play. There is a rest which corresponds in value to each type of note.

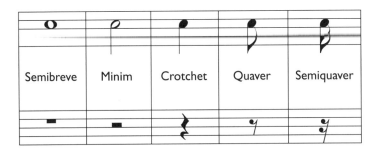

Semibreve	Minim	Crotchet	Quaver	Semiquaver

Similarly, dotted rests have the same time values as dotted notes.

A whole bar's rest is generally shown by a semibreve rest, whether or not the music is in 4/4 time.

Tablature explained

Guitarists often use a form of music notation called tablature, or TAB for short. It's a simplified form of notation, which shows pitch but doesn't provide information about rhythm or fingering. For this reason, classical guitarists use standard musical notation, but tablature can be useful as a back up, or 'easy' way to start playing.

The horizontal lines represent the strings of the guitar, going from bottom to top, so the top line of the tab is the top E string on the guitar. The numbers represent the frets, so for example a 3 would mean press the string at the third fret. Tab can also be used to show chords, by stacking numbers on top of one another.

1 Pluck the first string open, without fretting a note.

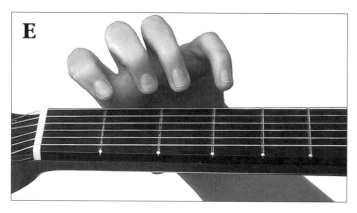

2 Press at the first fret and pluck that note (F).

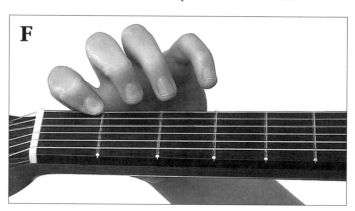

3 Press at the second fret and pluck that note (F#).

4 Finally, press at the third fret and pluck that note (G).

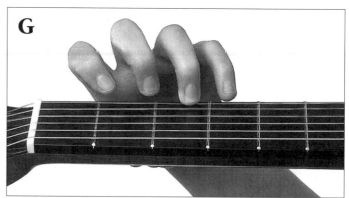

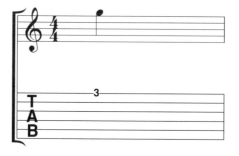

Here are some of the bits and pieces you'll want to equip yourself with as you progress with your playing.

Strings

Most important is a spare set of strings. You never know when they'll break! You should also change your strings periodically, depending on how often you play. There are three main types – for electric, acoustic and classical guitar.

Plectrum

We won't be using one in this book, but if your nails aren't long enough, you might want to try using one. They come in various thicknesses – start with a medium one.

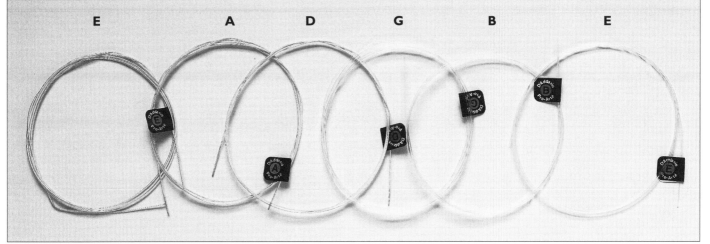

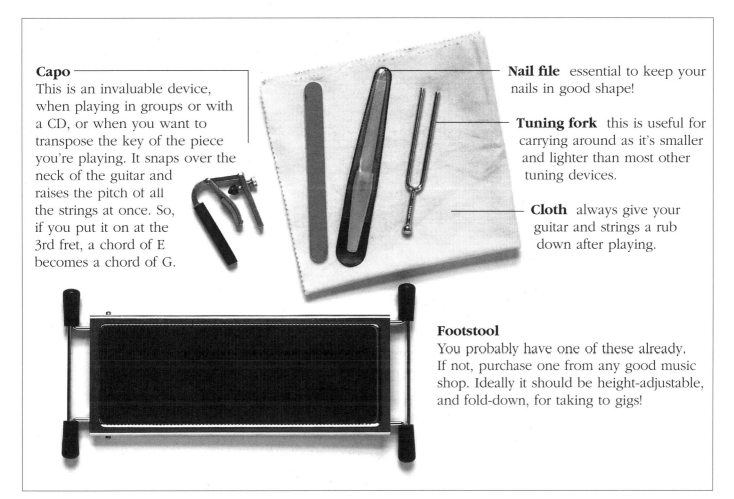

Capo

This is an invaluable device, when playing in groups or with a CD, or when you want to transpose the key of the piece you're playing. It snaps over the neck of the guitar and raises the pitch of all the strings at once. So, if you put it on at the 3rd fret, a chord of E becomes a chord of G.

Nail file essential to keep your nails in good shape!

Tuning fork this is useful for carrying around as it's smaller and lighter than most other tuning devices.

Cloth always give your guitar and strings a rub down after playing.

Footstool

You probably have one of these already. If not, purchase one from any good music shop. Ideally it should be height-adjustable, and fold-down, for taking to gigs!

The E string

Now it's time to start playing! You'll notice that there are some blank spaces on the music below. These are for you to fill in, a quick and easy way to become familiar with note names and tablature. Fill in the tab number in the white circle, and write the note name above it. All the notes you'll be playing on the E string are shown below for reference.

For the right hand, use alternating **i m** fingering, plucking first with the index and then the middle finger, using the free stroke.

Listen to the example on the CD a few times, then have a go yourself, starting slowly and building up speed. When you're ready, play along with the CD.

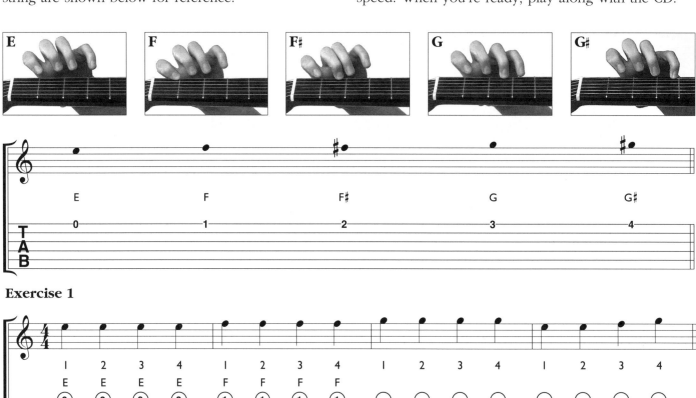

Exercise 1

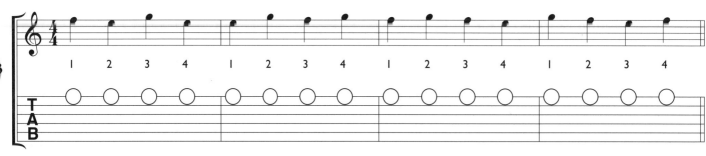

Track 2

Exercise 2

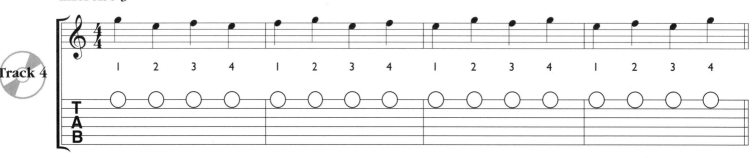

Track 3

Exercise 3

Track 4

Here are three more exercises, this time on the B string. With the notes on these two strings, you'll be able to start playing pieces.

Notice that on the second example the note heads are not filled in – these are **minims** (see pages 14-15) and should be played at half the speed of crotchets (the notes you've previously been playing).

On the third example, the notes are half as fast again, and are called **semibreves**. Basically, pluck the string and count to four before playing the next note.

Again, here are all the notes that you will be playing on the B string. Again, use alternating **i m** fingering.

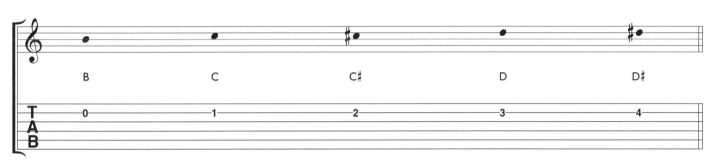

Exercise 1

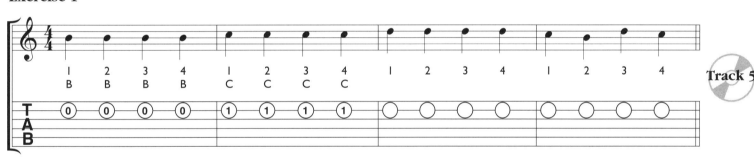

Track 5

Exercise 2

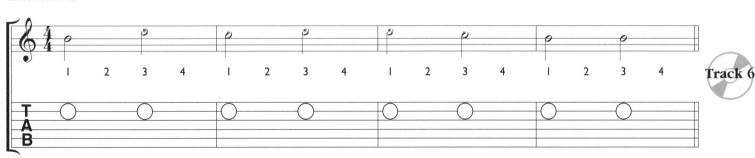

Track 6

Exercise 3

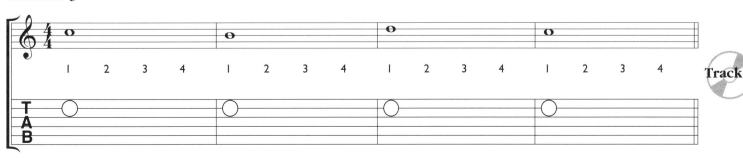

Track 7

Your first pieces!

Try these two easy pieces, designed to get you used to reading and playing from music and tab. Listen to the demonstration on track 8 and then, when you've practised it a few times, try playing along yourself with the backing track on track 9.

Track 8 Demonstration

Track 9 Backing Track

Merrily We Roll Along (Traditional)

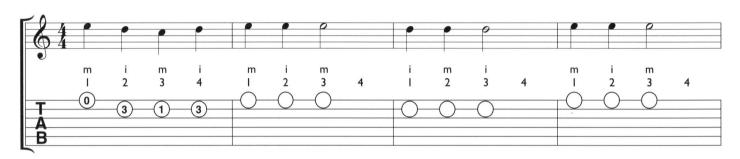

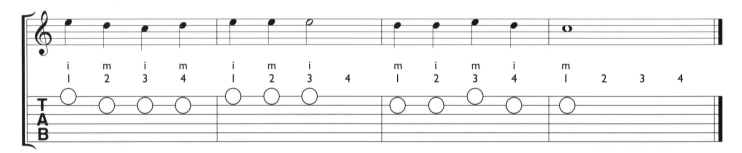

© Copyright 2003 Dorsey Brothers Music Limited.
All Rights Reserved. International Copyright Secured.

Track 10 Demonstration

Track 11 Backing Track

Go Tell Aunt Rhody (Traditional)

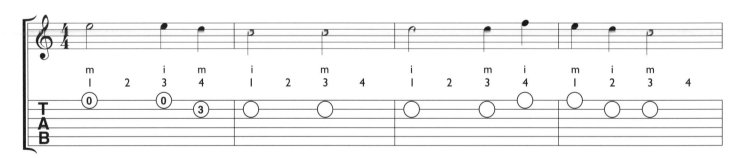

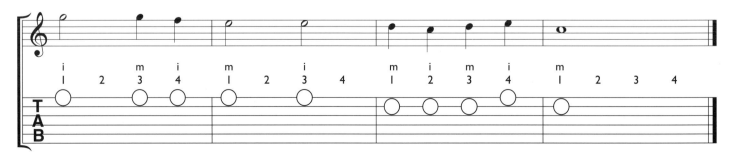

© Copyright 2003 Dorsey Brothers Music Limited.
All Rights Reserved. International Copyright Secured.

Here are all the notes that you will come across on the G string. In these exercises, we've used **repeat signs** – that's the two vertical lines with dots at the end of each exercise, and means that you should repeat everything within the repeat signs once, or from the beginning.

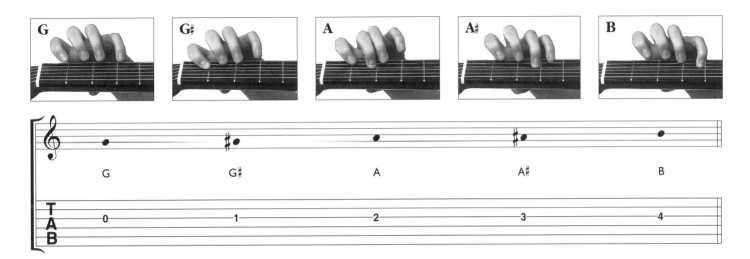

Exercise 1

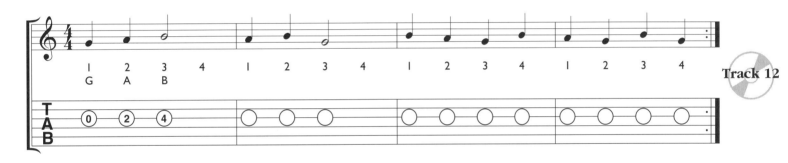

Track 12

Exercise 2

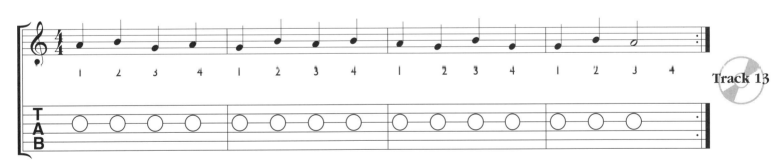

Track 13

Exercise 3

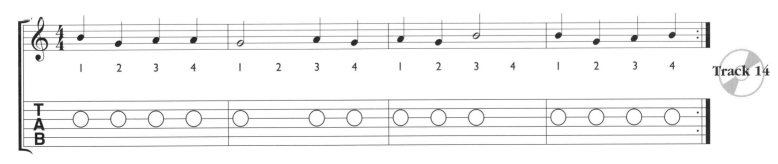

Track 14

Ode To Joy

This piece is the theme from Beethoven's Ninth Symphony, and you will probably recognise it.

Don't worry about the chord symbols (the letters in bold above the music) – you will learn about chords later, but if you have a friend who wants to accompany you, they can use these.

Track 15 Demonstration

Track 16 Backing Track

Symphony No.9 OP.125 by Ludwig van Beethoven

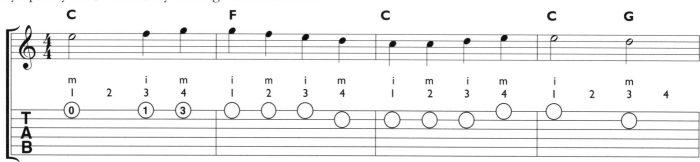

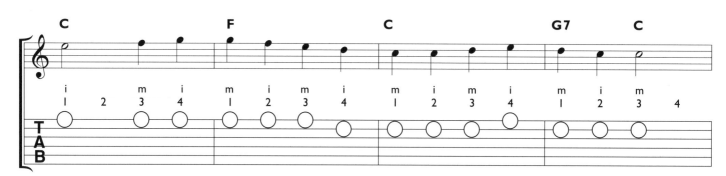

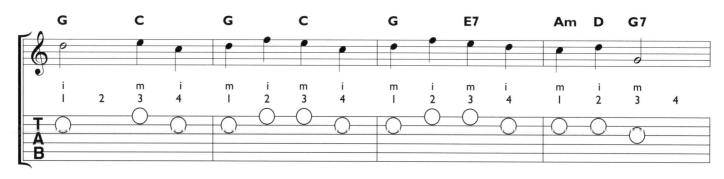

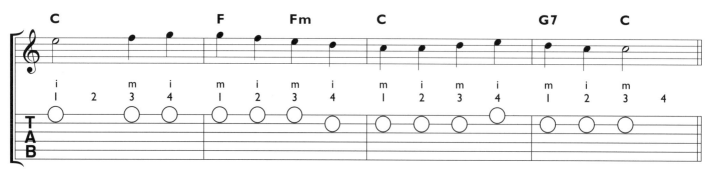

Here's another easy piece using the E, B and G strings. This piece uses a new time signature, 3/4, which basically means 3 beats in the bar instead of 4, and gives it a 'lilting' feel. The other thing to look out for is dotted notes. They add half the note's value to it, so a dotted minim becomes a three-beat instead of two-beat note (see page 15 for more).

Track 17 Demonstration

Track 18 Backing Track

Waltz OP.127 No.18   by Franz Schubert

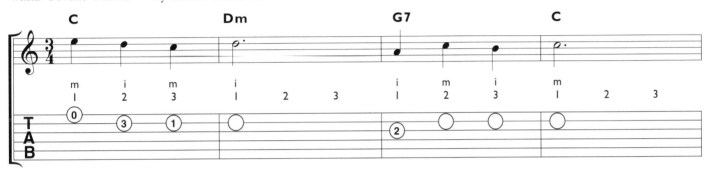

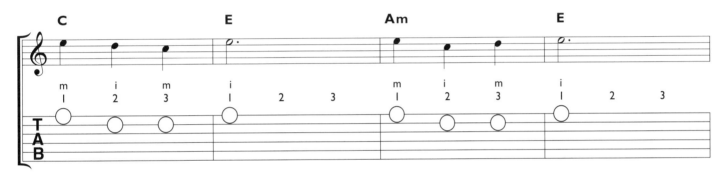

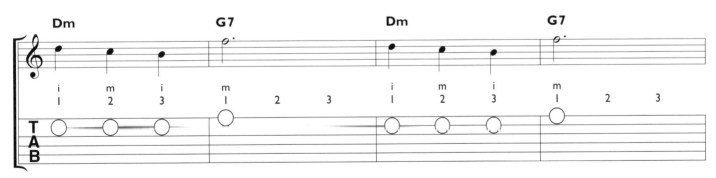

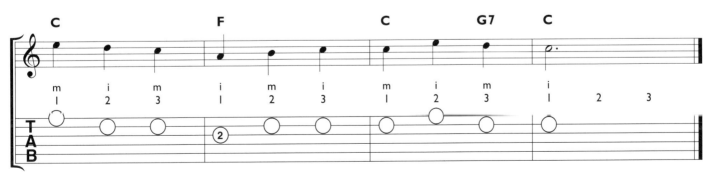

Scarborough Fair

This piece is also in 3/4 time so remember to count 3 beats in each bar. Also, in bar 7 you will see a ♯ (sharp) symbol. This indicates that the note should be raised by a semi-tone, or one fret. So instead of playing the first fret note (F) you should play the second fret note (F♯). This note is shown on page 18.

Track 19 Demonstration

Track 20 Backing Track

Traditional

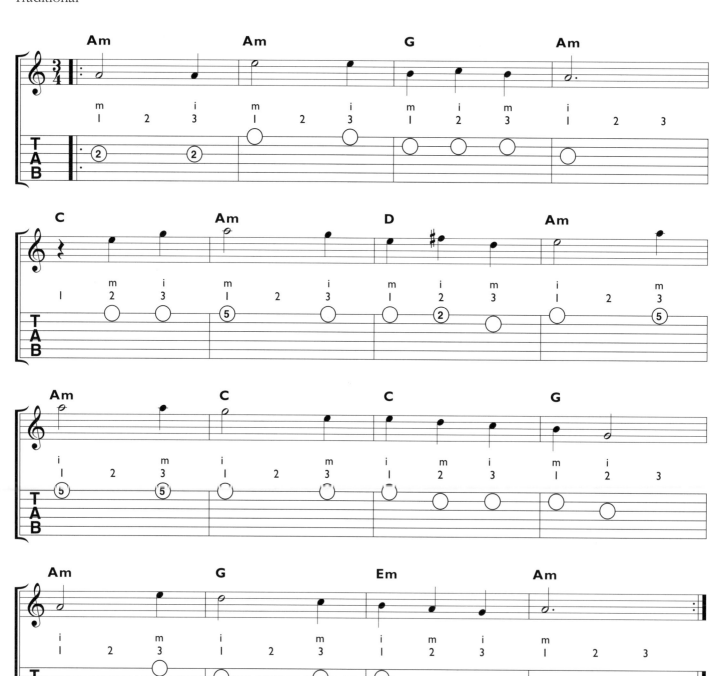

Here's your first chance to play quavers, or eighth-notes. As you'll remember from page 15, these are twice the speed of crotchets, or quarter-notes. They can be a little tricky to play – so make sure you take this slowly to start with, and remember to count! Also in this piece is a ♭ (flat) symbol – in bar 13. This is the opposite of a sharp and means lower the note by a semi-tone, making that note on the fourth fret of the B string, instead of on the open E string.

It also applies to every E note in that bar, but is cancelled out by the bar line.

Track 21 Demonstration

Track 22 Backing Track

By Franz Schubert

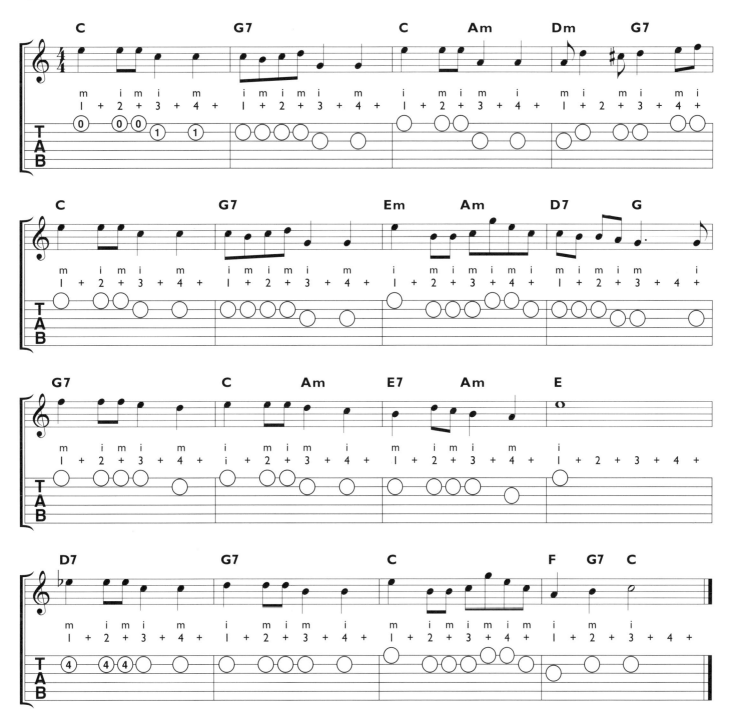

The **D** string

Here are all the notes that you will come across on the D string. As with all the exercises, play these steadily, and keep counting all the way through.

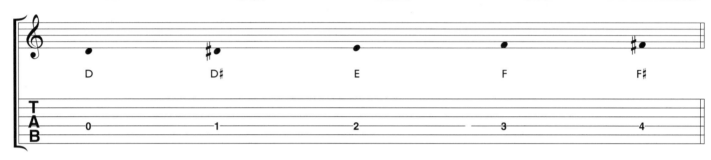

Exercise 1

Track 23

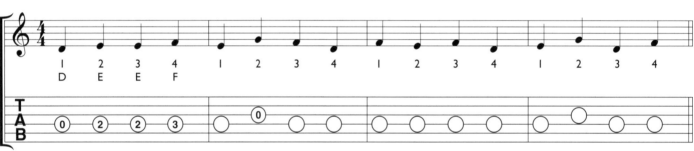

Exercise 2

Track 24

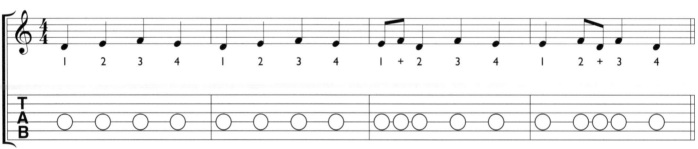

Exercise 3

Track 25

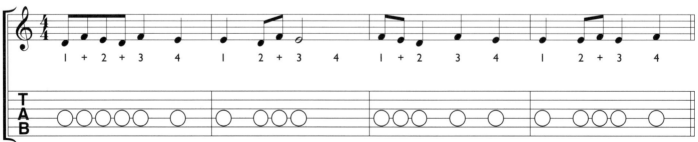

Here we have some more repeat signs. Bars 1-4 should be played twice, then continue on to bar 5. Then play everything between bars 9-12 twice, and continue on to bar 13 to finish. Keep an eye out for the sharp signs too! Use the free stroke here.

Track 26 Demonstration

Track 27 Backing Track

Traditional

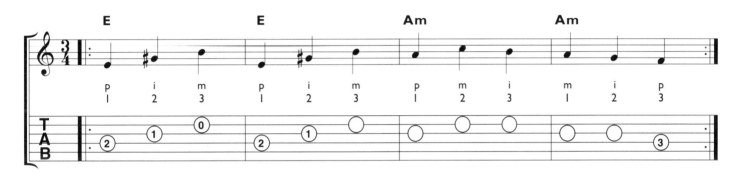

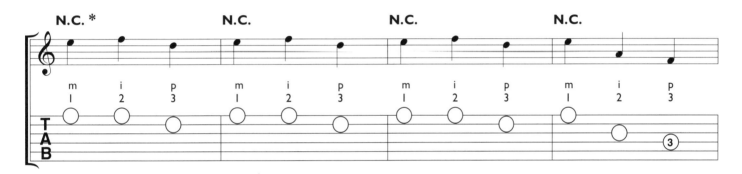

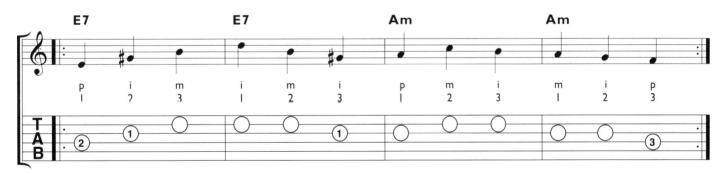

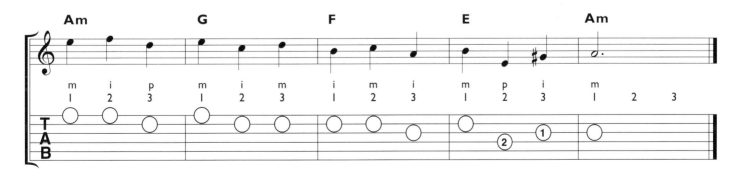

*N.C. = no chord

La Paloma

This piece starts on the last beat of the bar, so after the normal 2 bar click count 1, 2, 3 and start on 4.

Track 28 Demonstration

Track 29 Backing Track

In bars 12-13, a curved line, called a **tie**, links two G notes. A tie adds one notes' value to the other – so play the G, then hold for four beats.

By Sebastian Yradier

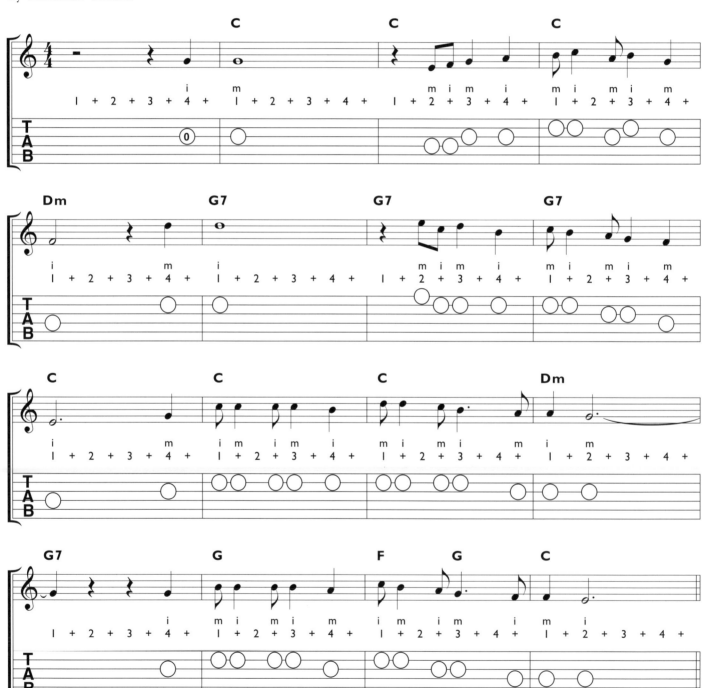

Here's another piece in 3/4 time, which also uses dotted notes and quavers! When playing dotted notes, the most important thing to remember is counting. Follow the counting patterns below the music for help on when to play. Look out for the **accidentals** (sharps and flats) in bars 6 and 12.

Track 30 Demonstration

Track 31 Backing Track

Traditional

The **A** string

Here are all the notes that you will come across on
the A string. Notice how the notes sit on little extra
lines below the stave – these are called **ledger lines**.
They are used to show the pitch of notes which lie
beyond the range of the stave, either higher or lower.

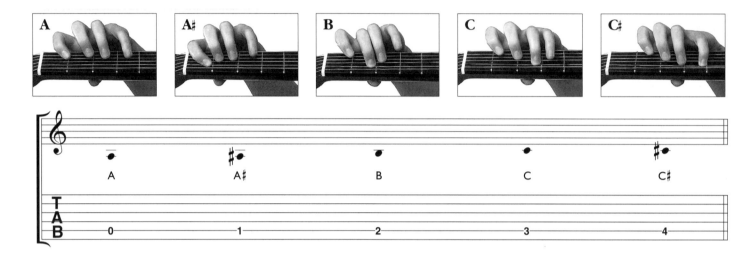

Exercise 1

Track 32

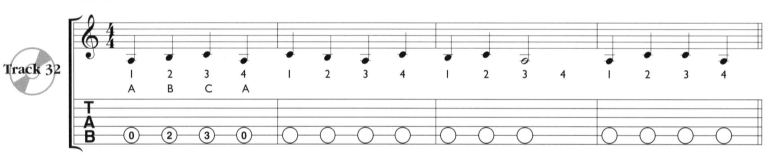

Exercise 2

Track 33

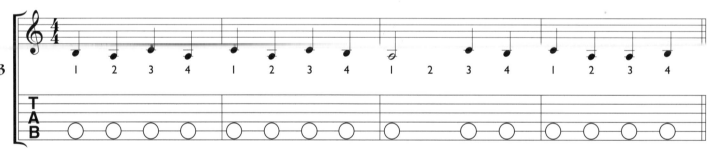

Exercise 3

Track 34

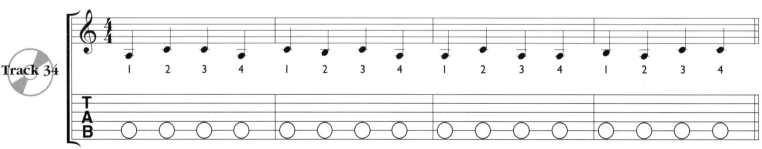

In bars 4 and 14 of this piece, we've shown some finger numbers in the music for the left hand. This is common in classical guitar music, and is a suggestion of the easiest way of playing it – however, if you find a better way, use it!

There are a lot of accidentals in this piece, and also look out for the **pause** in bar 14 ($\frown$) – hold the note for a few seconds and then continue to the end.

Track 35 Demonstration

Track 36 Backing Track

By Francisco Tarrega

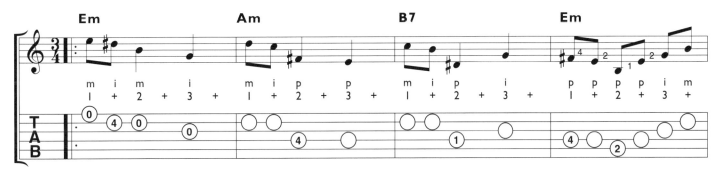

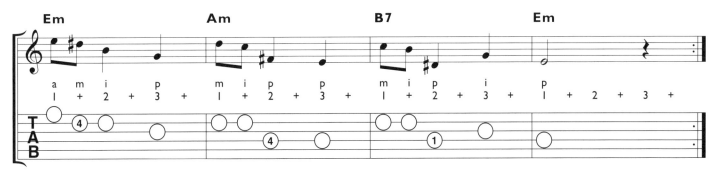

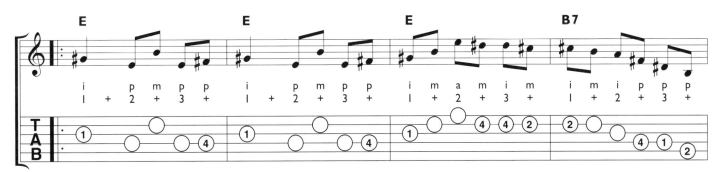

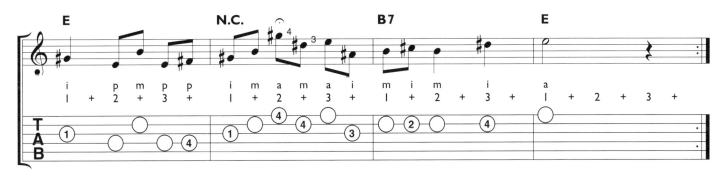

O Sole Mio

Here's another well-known tune for you to play. There's plenty to look out for in this piece, such as quavers, sharps and ties. Also, you should play the first 16 bars with the thumb, then change to alternating **i m** fingering for the second 16 bars. Listen to the demonstration, practise by yourself slowly, and then try playing along with the backing track.

Track 37 Demonstration

Track 38 Backing Track

Words by Giovanni Capurro
Music by Edorado di Capua

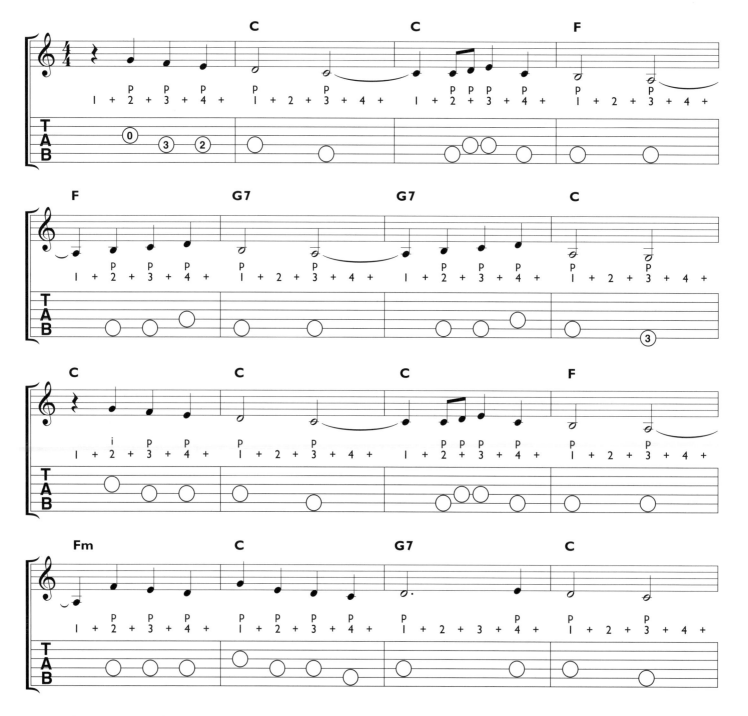

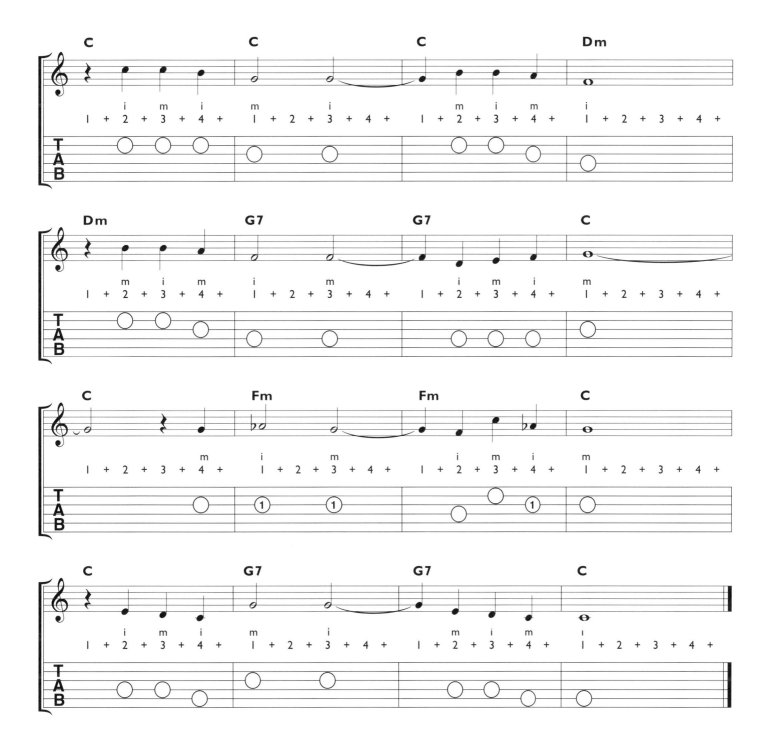

The E string

Here are all the notes that you will come across on the bottom E string. Again, ledger lines need to be used to show the notes as they are too low for the stave. Repeat all of the exercises on this page.

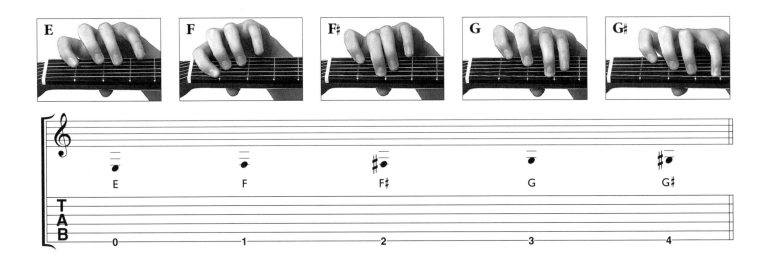

Exercise 1

Track 39

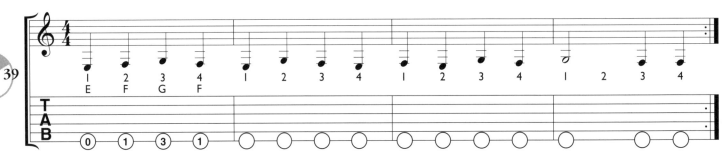

Exercise 2

Track 40

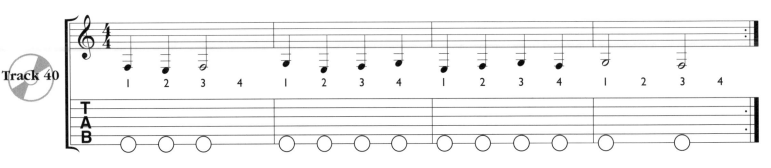

Exercise 3

Track 41

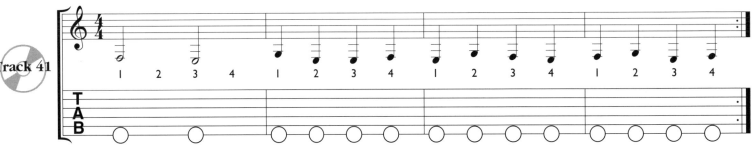

Nocturne Op.9 No.2

This Chopin Nocturne is probably better known as a piano piece, but is equally playable on guitar. The piece is in an 'accompaniment' style, where you play notes of the accompanying chord as well as the melody. The piano on the backing track plays the melody – see if you can spot it. Then, accent the melody notes, playing the 'accompaniment' notes slightly softer. Use the free stroke to play this piece.

Watch out for the **anacrusis** – this means that the piece starts on the last beat of the bar, instead of the first. Count 1, 2, and then play on beat 3.

Track 42 Demonstration

Track 43 Backing Track

By Frederic Chopin

El Condor Pasa

There are lots of quavers in this piece – keep a steady rhythm going. There is a suggested fingering at bar 12-13, and 16-17, and a repeat at the end, so play the whole piece again. This piece also starts on the last beat of the bar, so count 1, 2, 3 and start on beat 4.

Track 44 Demonstration

Track 45 Backing Track

Traditional

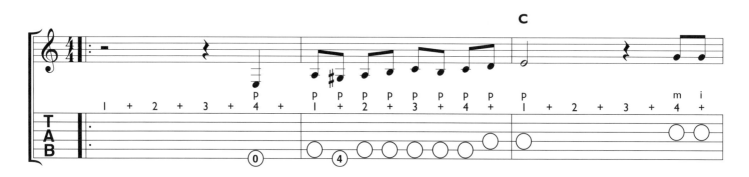

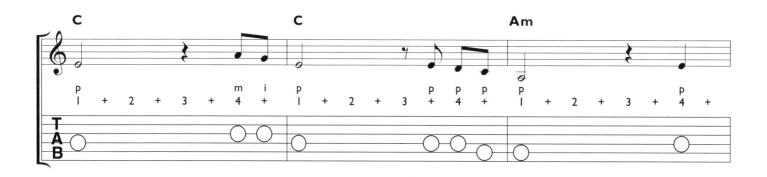

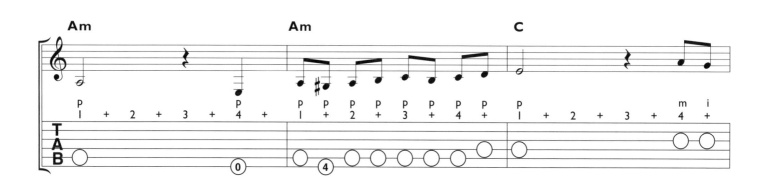

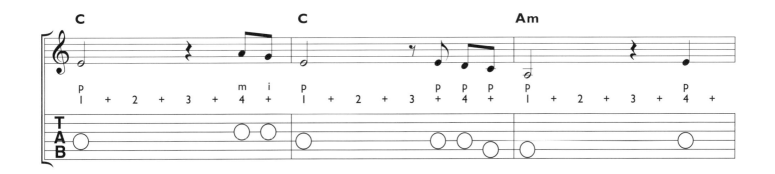

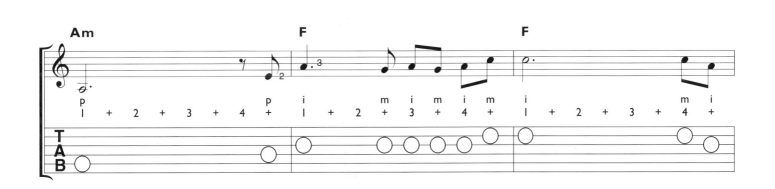

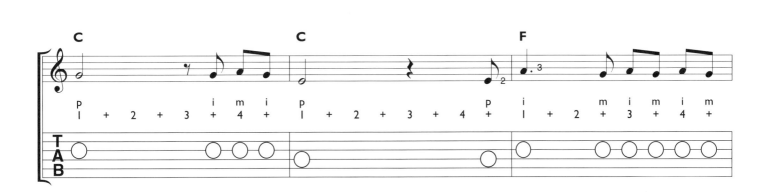

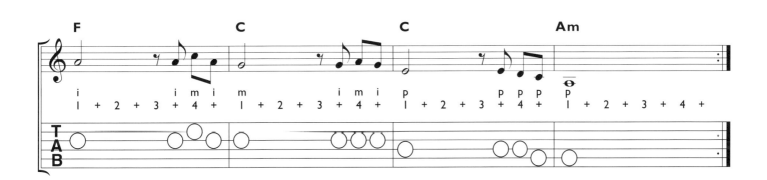

Spanish Romanza

Here's another piece in 3/4 time, with straightforward crotchets all the way through – play with your thumb. Why not also try some accompaniments using chords – see pages 44-46 for all the chord shapes. Fret the chord, then alternate between thumb and fingers to create an 'arpeggio' fingerstyle accompaniment, or use one of the accompaniment styles on page 41.

Track 46 Demonstration

Track 47 Backing Track

Traditional

This piece should also be played with your thumb all the way through. It's quite fast and probably the most challenging piece in the book, so take your time. The harmony is based on Am and E chords, so again, you could try making up an arpeggio-based accompaniment using these chords.

Track 48 Demonstration

Track 49 Backing Track

From Suite Española by Isaac Albeniz

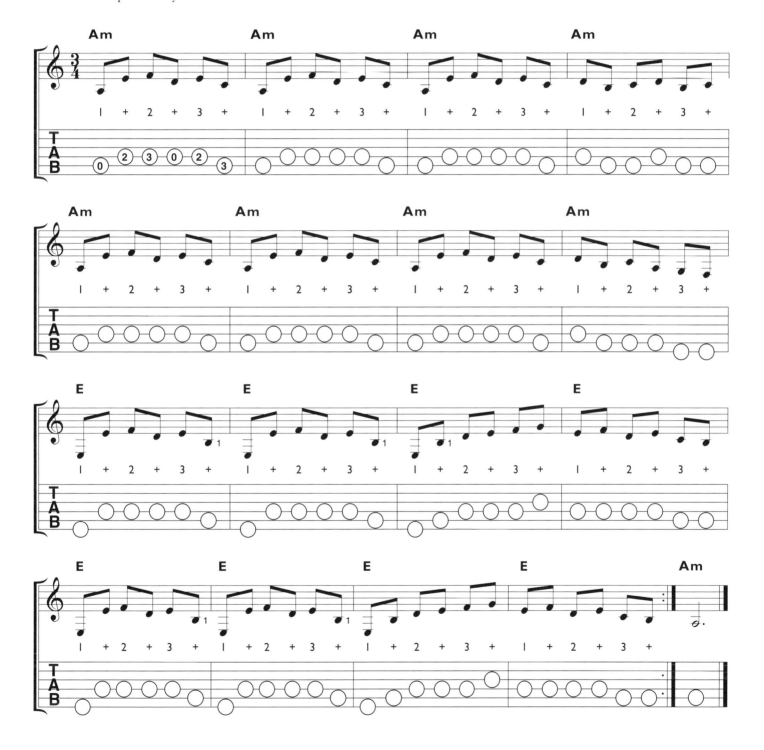

La Cumparista

This piece features slow bass notes, with a melody above. The two lines are treated as separate in the music, which is why rests appear above the bass notes – they are part of the higher line. Use your thumb again here, except where fingerings appear in the music.

Track 50 Demonstration

Track 51 Backing Track

Traditional

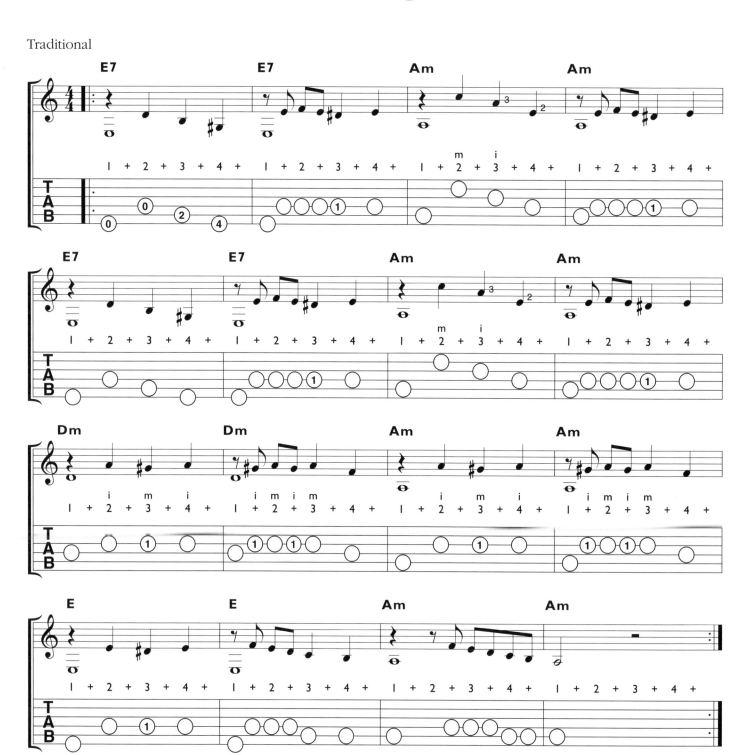

Here are four different fingerstyle patterns that you can use to make up accompaniments to songs. They have all been based on a chord of E minor.

When playing accompaniments, you could stick to the same pattern all the way through, or you could alternate, or even make up some of your own.

Fingerstyle pattern 1

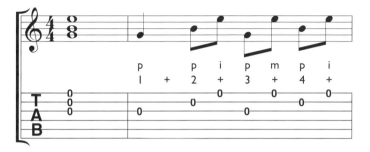

Fingerstyle pattern 2

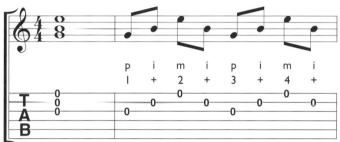

Fingerstyle pattern 3

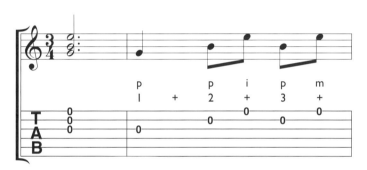

Fingerstyle pattern 4

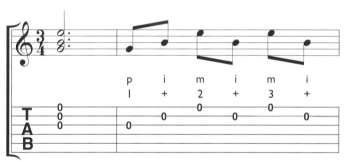

Note finder

Below on the left is a reference to all the notes you've learned on the guitar. On the right is a diagram of the fretboard with all the notes marked.

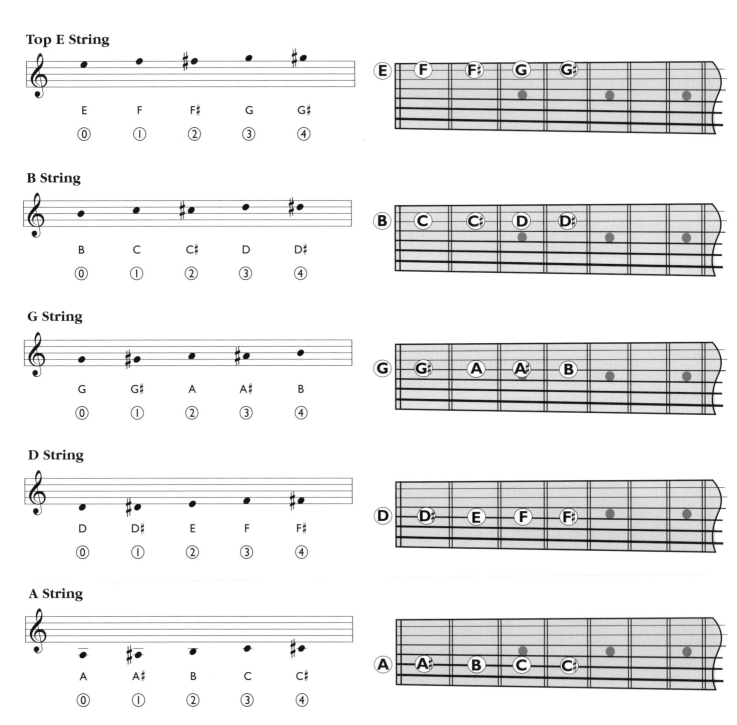

Top E String

E F F# G G#
0 1 2 3 4

B String

B C C# D D#
0 1 2 3 4

G String

G G# A A# B
0 1 2 3 4

D String

D D# E F F#
0 1 2 3 4

A String

A A# B C C#
0 1 2 3 4

E String

E F F# G G#
0 1 2 3 4

Here are two diagrams to help you learn all the note names on the guitar fretboard. The diagram on the left shows the note names using flats, the diagram on the right shows the note names using sharps.

However, they are the same notes – every sharp has an equivalent flat (for instance C♯ is the same as D♭). It is important to remember this as you will come across some songs that use sharp notes while others use flats.

You will also notice that the note names run in repeating patterns or sequences. This is because there are only twelve notes in an **octave**, which is two notes with the same name but at different pitches (one higher than the other).

Remember that a sharp (♯) symbol **raises** the pitch of the note by one semitone (which is one fret on your guitar), and a flat symbol (♭) **lowers** the pitch in the same way.

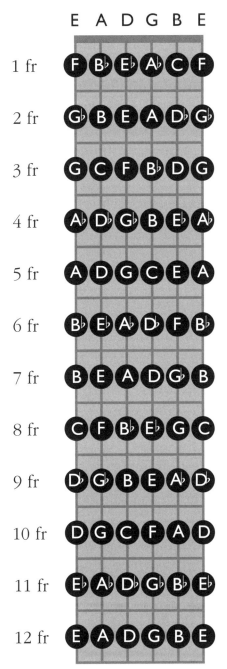

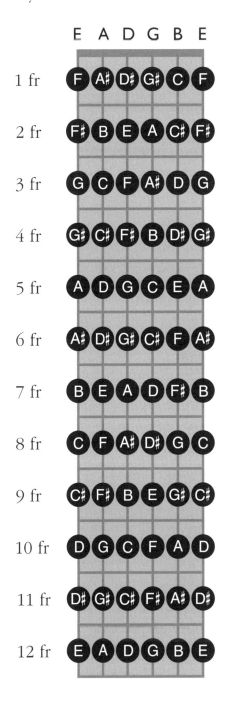

Use this diagram if you want to find a note with a **flat** in its name.

Use this diagram if you want to find a note with a **sharp** in its name.

Chord finder

Here are chord shapes for all the chords used in the songs in this book. These simplified triad (or 3-note) chords require only the top three strings, and are shown using chord boxes and tab.

How to read chord boxes

The bottom E string is on the left, and the top E string is on the right. The strings run vertically and the frets horizontally. An 'x' above a string indicates that you should not play that string. An 'o' above a string indicates an open string. The numbers in circles refer to which finger you should use to fret the note.

A minor

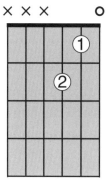
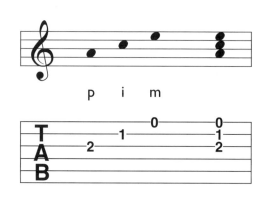

D minor

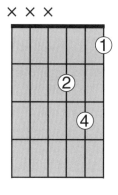
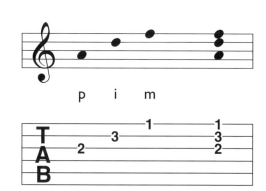

E minor

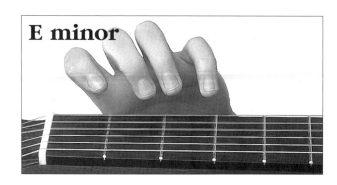
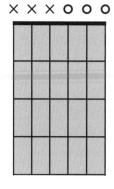
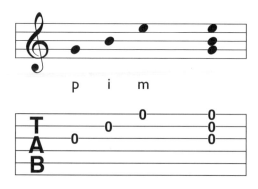

F minor

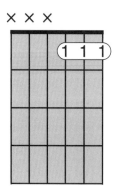
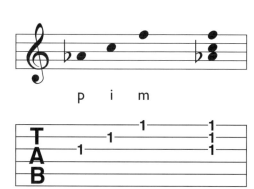

G major

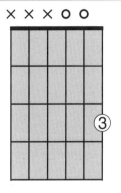
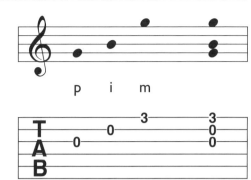

C major

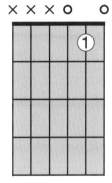
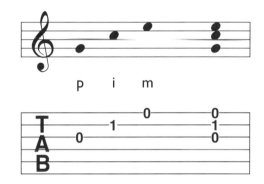

D major

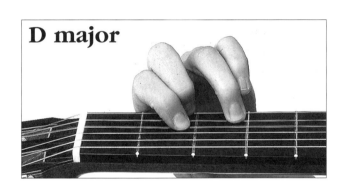
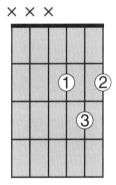

E major

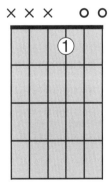
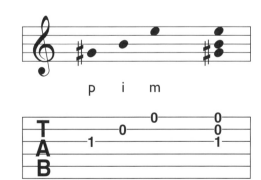

F major

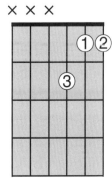
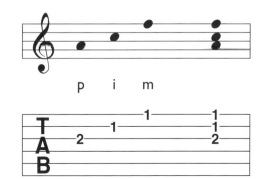

Chord finder

A7

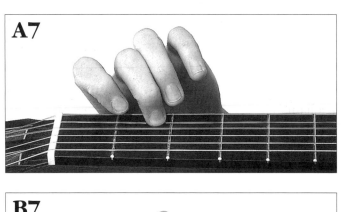 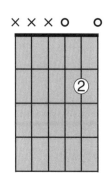 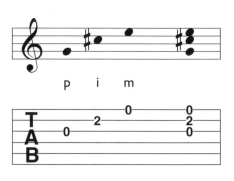

B7

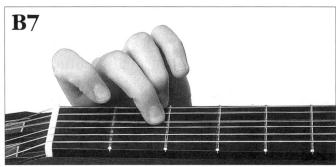 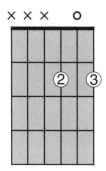 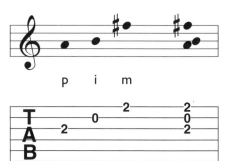

D7

 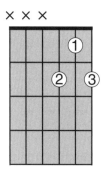 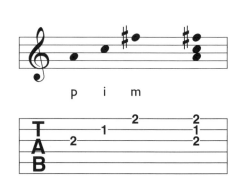

E7

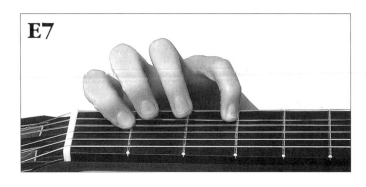 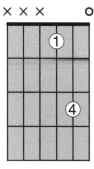 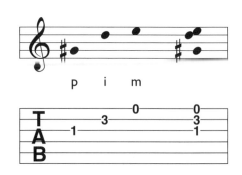

G7

 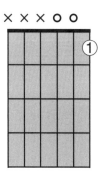 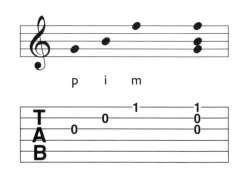

Congratulations! If you've made it this far, you're now ready to move on to more advanced material. I hope you've enjoyed playing through this book and that you will feel inspired to carry on learning and playing classical guitar. Whether you'd like to play more pieces, or continue improving your technique, take a look at the selection below, available from your local music shop.

Tutorials

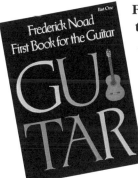

Frederick Noad's First Book for the Guitar

A beginner's manual to the classical guitar and its literature in a systematic approach, utilising solo and duet music. Three-book series, to progress from complete beginner to competent player.
GS33437

The Complete Guitar Player Classical Book

Russ Shipton's best-selling tutorial for the guitar, ideal for beginners. Uses easy-to-follow instructions, diagrams and photographs, and well-known pieces, with a CD.
AM38217

A Tune A Day for Classical Guitar

Concentrates on the acquisition of a musical background and a solid technical foundation.
Two-book series.
BM10124

Repertoire books

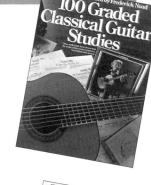

100 Graded Classical Guitar Studies

Music from Carcassi, Sor and Giuliani. With study and performance notes on each piece.
AM38597

The Classic Guitar Collection

Outstanding solos for the classical guitar from the fourteeth century to Bartok. Includes works by Bach, Carcassi, Giuliani, Mozart, Shostakovich and Sor. Three volumes available.
AM32657

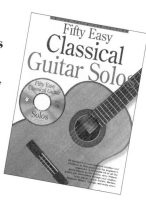

Fifty Easy Classical Guitar Solos

Fifty gems for the beginner's repertoire by Sor, Aguago, Mozart, Carulli, Dowland and De Visée. Accompanying CD contains full length performances.
AM949058

Pop Hits for Classical Guitar

Provides classical players with an opportunity to extend their repertoire with some popular hit songs. Includes '(Everything I Do) I Do It For You', 'Tears In Heaven' and 'Wonderwall'.
AM92625

Guitar Music of Cuba

A unique collection of traditional and well-known Cuban guitar music. Includes 'Habañera' (Bizet), 'La Comparsa' (Lecuona), 'Cachita' (Hernandez) and 'The Peanut Vendor' (Simons).
CH61433
Also available: **Guitar Music of Argentina CH61434**
Guitar Music of Brazil CH61421

CD track list

Track 1	Tuning Notes
Track 2	The E string – Exercise 1
Track 3	The E string – Exercise 2
Track 4	The E string – Exercise 3
Track 5	The B string – Exercise 1
Track 6	The B string – Exercise 2
Track 7	The B string – Exercise 3
Track 8	**Merrily We Roll Along** demonstration
Track 9	**Merrily We Roll Along** backing track
Track 10	**Go Tell Aunt Rhody** demonstration
Track 11	**Go Tell Aunt Rhody** backing track
Track 12	The G string – Exercise 1
Track 13	The G string – Exercise 2
Track 14	The G string – Exercise 3
Track 15	**Ode To Joy** demonstration
Track 16	**Ode To Joy** backing track
Track 17	**Waltz** demonstration
Track 18	**Waltz** backing track
Track 19	**Scarborough Fair** demonstration
Track 20	**Scarborough Fair** backing track
Track 21	**Theme from Rosamunde** demonstration
Track 22	**Theme from Rosamunde** backing track
Track 23	The D string – Exercise 1
Track 24	The D string – Exercise 2
Track 25	The D string – Exercise 3
Track 26	**Cyclic Flamenco** demonstration
Track 27	**Cyclic Flamenco** backing track
Track 28	**La Paloma** demonstration
Track 29	**La Paloma** backing track
Track 30	**Santa Lucia** demonstration
Track 31	**Santa Lucia** backing track
Track 32	The A string – Exercise 1
Track 33	The A string – Exercise 2
Track 34	The A string – Exercise 3
Track 35	**Adelita** demonstration
Track 36	**Adelita** backing track
Track 37	**O Sole Mio** demonstration
Track 38	**O Sole Mio** backing track
Track 39	The E string – Exercise 1
Track 40	The E string – Exercise 2
Track 41	The E string – Exercise 3
Track 42	**Nocturne Op.9 No.2** demonstration
Track 43	**Nocturne Op.9 No.2** backing track
Track 44	**El Condor Pasa** demonstration
Track 45	**El Condor Pasa** backing track
Track 46	**Spanish Romanza** demonstration
Track 47	**Spanish Romanza** backing track
Track 48	**Asturias** demonstration
Track 49	**Asturias** backing track
Track 50	**La Cumparista** demonstration
Track 51	**La Cumparista** backing track

9 10 11 12 13 14 15 16 17 18 19